W9-ALM-007

Safety First!

Safety at the Swimming Pool

by Lucia Raatma

Bridgestone Books
an imprint of Capstone Press
Mankato, Minnesota

J797.2?
RAA

Bridgestone Books are published by Capstone Press
818 North Willow Street, Mankato, Minnesota 56001
http://www.capstone-press.com

Copyright © 1999 Capstone Press. All rights reserved.
No part of this book may be reproduced without written permission from the publisher.
The publisher takes no responsibility for the use of any of the materials
or methods described in this book, nor for the products thereof.
Printed in the United States of America.

Library of Congress Cataloging-in-Publication Data
Raatma, Lucia.
    Safety at the swimming pool/by Lucia Raatma.
    p. cm.—(Safety first!)
    Includes bibliographical references (p. 24) and index.
    Summary: Discusses the safety aspects of swimming in a public pool,
including such topics as having a buddy, listening to the lifeguards, shallow
and deep water, diving boards, and emergencies.
    ISBN 0-7368-0191-X
    1. Swimming—Safety measures—Juvenile literature. 2. Swimming for
children—Safety measures—Juvenile literature. [1. Swimming—Safety
measures. 2. Safety.] I. Title. II. Series: Raatma, Lucia. Safety first.
GV838.53.S24R33 1999
797.2'1'083—dc21   98-45319
                                                         CIP
                                                         AC

Editorial Credits

Rebecca Glaser, editor; Steve Christensen, cover designer; Kimberly Danger,
    photo researcher

Photo Credits

Chris Salvo/FPG International LLC, cover
David F. Clobes, 4, 6, 8, 10, 16, 18, 20
James L. Shaffer, 12, 14

**Bridgestone Books wishes to thank Laura Slane, associate director, product
development, aquatics, of the YMCA of the USA for reviewing this material.**

10.95

Table of Contents

Pool Rules 5

Swim with a Buddy 7

Sunscreen 9

Lifeguards 11

Shallow and Deep Water 13

Other Swimmers 15

Diving Boards 17

Emergencies at the Pool 19

When to Get Out 21

Hands On: Who Can Float Longer? 22

Words to Know 23

Read More 24

Internet Sites 24

Index 24

POOL RULES

1. WALK, DON'T RUN.
2. DO NOT DIVE INTO MAIN POOL.
3. NO DUNKING OR HORSEPLAY IN OR AROUND POOL.
4. DO NOT SPLASH OR VISIT WITH LIFEGUARDS.
5. NO SMOKING, EATING, OR CHEWING GUM IN POOL AREA. POP MUST BE KEPT IN TABLE AREA.
6 2 LOUD BLASTS ON WHISTLE MEANS CLEAR POOL.

Pool Rules

Staying safe is the best way to enjoy the swimming pool. You can be safe if you follow pool rules. Do not run near the pool. You could slip and fall. Never eat or chew gum while you swim. You could choke. Always ask an adult to watch you while you swim.

Sunscreen

The sun's rays can burn your skin. Apply waterproof sunscreen on your skin before you get wet. Ask an adult to rub sunscreen on your back. Apply sunscreen often while you are at the pool.

sunscreen

a lotion that protects your skin from the sun; waterproof sunscreen will not wash off in water.

Lifeguards

Lifeguards watch swimmers at the pool. Lifeguards make sure everyone swims and plays safely. They help swimmers in emergencies. Listen to lifeguards and follow pool rules. If you do not, lifeguards may ask you to leave the pool.

emergency

a sudden danger; an emergency at the pool might be someone drowning.

11

Shallow and Deep Water

Read the numbers along the pool edge before you get in the pool. Low numbers mean the water is shallow. Never dive into shallow water. You could hit your head. High numbers mean the water is deep. Do not jump into deep water unless you are a good swimmer.

Other Swimmers

Swimming pools can be crowded. Keep out of the way of other swimmers. Do not push people. Do not swim under diving boards. People could land on you when they dive. Do not swim near ladders. People climbing into the pool may not see you.

Diving Boards

Diving boards can be fun. But you must learn to use them safely. Take your time on diving boards. Wait until the person in front of you dives. Then slowly walk out to the end of the board. Do not dive until the first diver swims away from the board.

Emergencies at the Pool

Call for a lifeguard or another adult if there is an emergency. Do not try to save people who are drowning. They could pull you underwater too. Ask a lifeguard or an adult to help.

When to Get Out

You should know when to get out of the pool. Get out and rest if you are cold or tired. You might not swim as well if you are cold or tired. Get out of the pool if there is bad weather. Swimming is not safe when lightning flashes in the sky.

Hands On: Who Can Float Longer?

You should always swim with a buddy. You may get tired if you swim for a long time. It is easier to float than to swim if you are tired. You and your buddy can practice floating.

What You Need

Buddy
Waterproof stopwatch or a watch with a second hand

What You Do

1. Enter the water at the shallow end of the pool.
2. Ask your buddy to time you with the stopwatch or clock.
3. Start floating. Your buddy should start timing as soon as you start floating.
4. See how long you can float before your feet touch the bottom.
5. Switch places with your buddy. Repeat steps one through four. Who can float longer?

Words to Know

buddy (BUHD-ee)—a friend or family member; you and your buddy watch out for each other when you swim.

emergency (i-MUR-juhn-see)—a sudden danger; an emergency at the pool might be someone drowning.

lifeguard (LIFE-gard)—a person trained to help swimmers

shallow (SHAL-oh)—not deep

sunscreen (SUHN-skreen)—a lotion that protects your skin from the sun; waterproof sunscreen will not wash off in water.

Read More

Carter, Kyle. *In Water.* Safety. Vero Beach, Fla.: Rourke, 1994.
Loewen, Nancy. *Water Safety.* Plymouth, Minn.: Child's World, 1997.

Internet Sites

AAP-TIPP—Water Safety for Your School-Age Child
http://www.aap.org/family/tipwater.htm
American Red Cross Water Safety Tips
http://www.redcross.org/news/common/96/watertip.html
OUPDS—Kid Safety
http://www.ou.edu/oupd/kidsafe/water.htm
Water Safety
http://www.cfc-efc.ca/docs/00000138.htm

Index

bad weather, 21
buddy, 7
diving boards, 15, 17
emergency, 11, 19
ladders, 15
lifeguards, 11, 19

lightning, 21
numbers, 13
pool, 5, 9, 11, 13, 15, 19, 21
rules, 5, 11
sunscreen, 9
swimmer, 11, 13, 15